Meet the Authors

Left to right:
Leo Dzuver, Alexander Hald and Matej Crnogorac

This book is For Grownups and Kids.

How to Get a Girlfriend

BY

Leo Dzuver

Alexander Hald
Matej Crnogorac

Scholastic Inc. New York Toronto London Auckland Sydney Mexico City New Delhi Hong Kong Buenos Aires

ORIGINAL COVER

For our SK friends and teachers

If you want a girlfriend, then you'll need to read this book.

5

First find a girl who you like. She has to be nice.

It doesn't matter what she looks like.

You need to brush your teeth. If you don't brush your teeth, she will think it is gross.

9

Have a shoLWer
So you Smell
good!

Don't
pick your nose
because she will
say "Yuck!"

13

Do Whatever She Wants. Don't do dangerous things!

15

Go to the toilet before you play so that you don't have to go while you are playing with her.

play with the girl a LOT and hug her.

Give her Flowers and toys.

Do a writing workShop So you can write her a Letter of LOVE.

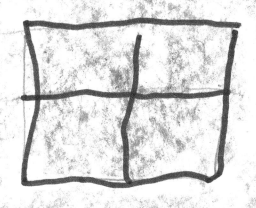

23

If you are
a grown up,
you can take
her to
the beach...

...or take her to a beautiful restaurant like a boat restaurant.

when you are a grownup, you can kiss, hug, go on trips, eat together, and be together.

It's fun to have a girlfriend because you can do lots of things with her and you can play with her.

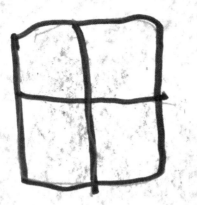

Kids Are Authors®
Books written by children for children

The Kids Are Authors® Competition was established in 1986 to encourage
children to read and to become involved in the creative process of writing.
Since then, thousands of children have written and illustrated books as
participants in the Kids Are Authors® Competition.

The winning books in the annual competition are published by Scholastic Inc.
and are distributed by Scholastic Book Fairs throughout the United States.

For more information:
Kids Are Authors® 1080 Greenwood Blvd., Lake Mary, FL 32746
Or visit our website at: www.scholastic.com/kidsareauthors

ISBN-978-0-545-80577-3
12 11 10 9 8 7 6 5 4 3 2

Cover design by Bill Henderson
Printed and bound in the U.S.A.
First Printing, June 2014